And The Mind Speaks
Thoughts on Life and Love

Volume 1

By

Jae Elle

Copyright © 2014 by Jae Elle, ATMS Inc.

All rights reserved. This book or any portion thereof may not be reproduced or used in any manner whatsoever without the express written permission of the publisher except for the use of brief quotations in a book review.

Printed in the United States of America

Second Edition, 2015

ISBN-13: 978-0692201466 (Custom)

ISBN-10: 0692201467

ATMS Publishing, Inc.

www.atmspeaks.com

Dedication

First and foremost I would like to thank God for giving me the gift of expression through words. This gift has allowed me to get through many of the most challenging times in my life. Next, I would like to dedicate this book to my parents. My parents have had a major influence on my life and witnessing their various successes has made me want to work even harder towards my own personal goals. To my friends and family, thank you. You have encouraged me to share my poems with the world and not to be afraid to take that leap into the unknown. Last, but certainly not least, to my fiancé, Marcus, you are appreciated. He has pushed me and supported me from day one. His love, support, and encouragement have been an awesome blessing and I am truly grateful that he has been with me through this entire experience.

Contents

INTRODUCTION 10

HEARTACHE 11

I Remember 13

My Team Player 16

Teddy Bear 19

Let's 22

You Have 24

LOVE 27

Paradise Lost 28

A Broken Dream 31

Screaming 33

What Is It That I'm Feeling? 36

Why I Loved You 38

LIFE 41

Our Children 42

Tick Tock 45

Emotionally Disconnected 48

A Revolution 52

A Beautiful Scar 55

INTIMACY 56

Explicit Content 58

Toxic 60

Oceans 61

Only Time Will Tell 63

Intimate Moment 64

HIS 67

Unemotional Woman 69

Loves A Man 71

I Want A Woman 73

My Man 75

Many Times 77

HERS 79

I Am That Type of Woman 81

A Choice 83

Can You See Me? 85

Visions 87

Untitled 90

JAE ELLE'S THOUGHTS 93

AFTERWARD 112

Introduction

To know one's dreams is, in turn, to know one's heart.............

  I came up with this quote when I started my blog, And The Mind Speaks, back in November of 2009. I created the blog so that people could read my poetry, thoughts, and opinions on various topics when it came to life and love. Even though a poetry book was what my ultimate goal was, I chose to do a blog because, in reality, I was afraid. I was terrified of the thought of putting my most intimate thoughts and feelings on display for so many to witness. It became even more daunting at the thought of being judged, or criticized, maybe even both. Because of this fear, I put off writing this book for six years. However, here I am, March of 2015 and I am finally re-publishing my first poetry book. I decided that I was no longer going to hide behind my fear of being judged, or criticized. I decided that I would no longer shy away because of the fear of failure. How can I fail at accomplishing a dream that I have always dreamt of? Not only am I publishing one book, which you are currently holding this very moment, but I will be publishing a second one next spring. And The Mind Speaks: Thoughts on Life and Love, Volume 1 is a collection of a few of my deepest and heartfelt works of poetry followed by some of my most colorful thoughts. I really hope that you enjoy every part of my poetry and get a more profound look into who I am.

Here we go...............

12

HEARTACHE

I Remember

I remember when he used to care,

when he used to caress my face.

I remember when he would hold my hand,

and smile at me as if he'd won first place.

I remember when we would lie in bed at night,

and he would hold me until I fell asleep.

I remember the key he gave me,

he said it was to his heart, and it was for me to keep.

I remember the first time he wiped away my tears,

and he tried so hard to make me laugh.

I remember those times I was tired, he cooked dinner,

lit candles, and ran me a bubble bath.

I remember when he first told me that he loved me,

I was too afraid to say it back.

I was afraid that if I spoke those words

It would set my heart up for attack.

I remember the smile on his face, when I saw him last.

I remember the smell of his cologne every time he would

walk pass.

I remember the sound of his laugh,

when we would joke around and play.

I remember the last words,

that he said to me that day.

He said, "Baby, you are my heart,

you mean the world to me.

Every time I am with you,

I feel as if I'm free.

You have all of the qualities any man would want,

that any man would need.

I can't see my life without you;

you bring out the best in me."

I never knew, that at that moment,

seeing his face, it would be my last.

Now he's gone away,

and his laughter is a distant past.

If only I would have said all of the things

that I intended to say,

if only I could have done

all of the things that I intended to do.

Now he's no longer here,

all I have are memories passed.

If you have a special someone

make sure they know exactly what's in your heart

and how much they mean to you,

or one day you may be the one sitting and saying

"I remember", too.

My Team Player

I thought that he was my team player

He never rode the bench.

He was my "go-to" guy,

the captain of my team.

He had ALL of the qualities of a star player and I,

I was his number one fan, his cheerleader,

and at times, maybe even his coach;

but most of all,

I was his teammate in our game of Love.

I dreamed about an eternity of Super Bowls,

but I guess his dream wasn't the same.

He was the Owner of my Team,

The Middle Linebacker of my Defense;

The Quarterback to my, ummm, Tight End.

But something happened.

Too many referees and umpires kept interrupting our playing time.

There were too many Time-Outs and Reviewing the Plays.

He began to Fumble the ball, my love,

too many times and there were never enough carries.

We haven't gained any Yardage.

My star player kept going Off Sides.

He was penalized for Illegal Contact, Personal Fouls, and Tripping.

Damn, too many women on the field.

What did I do? I kept him in the game. I reset the clock.

He, I felt, was my Safety, my chinstrap, my "mouth" guard.

I was willing to go into Sudden Death to keep that man. My man.

The first and second quarters have come and gone,

the half time show was a bust, and still no touchdown.

Not even a field goal.

How many red flags can a team take?

The 4-3 defense he ran didn't work.

He tried to switch to a 3-4 and it was a no-go.

He continued to throw Uncatchable Forward Passes,

and making Illegal Blocks on the field.

I had no choice. I had to call a Time-Out.

Why? Why do I continue to keep him in the game?

He can't even hold onto the ball.

He can't even keep my love safe and tucked away.

His un-sportsman like conduct keeps my heart sidelined.

We can't even reach our Neutral Zone.

I don't need a Line Judge to tell me the truth.

It's a Dead Ball and the play is over.

Stop the clock.

The game is done.

My Super Bowl ring is a distant thought.

Maybe next season.

4 quarters, 15 minutes each,

three hours, and I wanted a lifetime...

but I lost...I quit.

Teddy Bear: Metaphorically Speaking

I remember when I first noticed it,

The teddy bear that was mine.

I kept it close and treasured it,

and hid it all of the time.

I never thought much about having it,

until I was about 8.

Then this girl wanted it

and that's when innocence turned to hate.

Why did she insist on playing with mine,

when she had one of her own?

Why couldn't she just leave my teddy bear alone?

Four years she took my bear

and finally I stood up.

Leave MY Bear Alone,

but the damage had been done.

My bear had become slightly worn,

even though, on the outside, you couldn't tell.

I kept a smile on my face,

I'd learned to wear it well.

At sixteen I was too old for a bear,

but I kept it near,

and this mean boy tried to tear it away

as I lay there shivering with fear.

Years passed and at 24,

I hid my teddy bear well.

I didn't let anyone too close to see it

They could hardly even tell.

But one night it was stolen,

I was helpless and terrified.

I didn't know why he wanted it,

why did he want mine?

The night he took my bear,

was the worst night of my life.

I probably could have fought him,

If it wasn't for the knife.

When he had played with it enough,

He quickly left my sight.

I sat crying in the dark,

afraid to sleep at night.

Let's

Let's think about what's real, what's true;

Let's think about all of the lies you told me

so that you could "do you".

Let's talk about what's real, what's true;

Let's talk about how much you hurt me

and whether, or not I should forgive you.

Let's wonder about what's real, what's true;

Let's wonder about how my heart will never

be able to look at you without a shattered view.

Let me tell you what's real;

Let me tell you what's true.

I hate what you've done to me.

I will never see the real you,

or maybe this you is true.

Now that you've broken my heart,

It is time for me to "do you".

You Have

You have a good thing staring you right in the face,

but you can't see it because you are so busy

looking past me, trying to see what's beyond.

You have a great thing staring you right in the eyes,

but you are so focused on the world's attention

that the universe which was given to you

has been pushed to the side.

You have a wonderful thing staring you right in the mouth,

yet your words don't bring forth the light

that your love needs to shine.

You have an amazing thing staring you right in the face,

however, you are so focused on the attention

of those who could not care any less about you,

that you just lost your future.

LOVE

Paradise Lost

As I lie in bed at night, clothed in my nakedness;

Cold sheets caressing my flesh wishing it was you.

Tears stain my pillow as I reach for you

and you are not there.

I close my eyes and fall

into your arms. The warmth of your

embrace

making me want to stay that way forever.

Your soft lips pressed against my ear as

you whisper

to me a lullaby.

The curvature of your body fitting

perfectly with mine.

As we melt into each other, seemingly

becoming one,

the intensity of our energy creating a

utopia of electricity.

The gravitational pull is so strong that it

makes the earth collapse around us.

Our force creates a sonic boom and our

world is created.

Our world, just me and you, you and I

in our own Secret Garden, our own

Secluded Island.

Your love is as blue as the ocean;

A never-ending abyss that I continuously

drown in.

Your fruit so delicious I never seem to

grow

tired of consuming….you

My thirst for your fluids is insatiable. I am

always

Wanting and needing more.

You will forever be…my Paradise Lost.

A Broken Dream

I lie back and I close my eyes...I wait....

I wait to see your beautiful face.

Sometimes it comes and

then, sometimes is doesn't because....

I am in love with a Broken Dream.

I question my sanity when it comes to you

because I never know what to say, or

think.

I never know if I am coming, or going

because......

I am in love with a Broken Dream.

To wait in such a dark place brings

loneliness,

sometimes pain,

but those moments when you show up,

you bring a light that is so surreal,

so warming,

but unfortunately

I see more darkness than light because....

I am in love with a Broken Dream.

My dream is completely shattered.

It is slowly, but surely turning into a nightmare

yet still, I lie down, close my eyes

and I wait because...... I

am in love with a Broken Dream,

but yet,

I don't want to wake up.

Screaming

Each time I speak words, like bricks, they

break as they hit the earth, left alone to

crumble.

I stumble, you fall,

but through it all I catch myself.

Just for you, your sound,

Blood-curdling screams speak life

as I die in the wake of a mirage of

happiness.

Let loves grip of hatred pour out a sweet

kiss of selfishness.

The glares as I sleep in the sea of

forgetfulness.

I breathe in the scent of hope

as it slips through my fingers.

Tears stain my face as my flesh burns

away

and the bone is exposed.

This is I, unclothed.

My soul naked and bare for you

and the world to see. I scream and

I claw at my mind, digging for the right

words to say.

As I continue to dig my fingers are

reduced to nubs.

How far do I need to go?

How much further shall I dig?

My vision starts to fade and I see black.

I hear the voices,

but I am blinded by my own demons.

Demons fed by you and your insecurities

and lies.

Expectations that falsely bind our spirits

into one.

I scream out....

We die together, we are resurrected

together,

we bleed and bruise together,

yet we love.....together.

What Is It That I Am Feeling?

What is it that I am feeling?

This beating in my chest...

I feel my blood running through my veins;

I feel double tapping beneath my breasts.

The sound of something in my heart,

something foreign, something new;

The sound of something in my heart,

That unfamiliar feeling....is you...

However foreign you may seem,

whatever this is that I am feeling

takes on a familiar face;

My blood and your blood have joined

together

inside..... my space.....

Our face, our book, in an instant the

grams, the

weight we share causes me to be linked in

to you..

What is it that I am feeling?

This beating in my chest...

It is the beating of both of our

hearts together...underneath my breasts?

Why I Loved You

You asked me why I loved you,

I said it was your smile.

You asked me why I loved you,

I replied, "You drive my soul

completely wild."

You asked me why I love you,

I answered, "Baby, it's your honesty."

You asked me why I loved you,

I told you, "Because you let me, be me."

You asked me why I loved you,

I said, "It's because you keep

it real."

You asked me why I loved you,

I replied, "Sweetheart, it's just

the way that you make me feel."

You asked me why I loved you,

I answered, "Honey, you hold my heart."

You asked me why I loved you,

I told you, "You are my light when it

gets dark."

You asked me why I loved you,

Finally I said,

"I can tell you why I love you,

but they all would be a lie,

truth be told I love you,

far beyond the question why."

LIFE

Our Children

Young minds are being molded everyday inside the walls

of America's education system.

Many children playing the roles of heroes

when some of them truly are the victim.

For some, they welcome the security of this institution.

It provides a safe haven for them

compared to their living conditions.

They have warm food to put into their tummies

and for a few hours, a normal existence.

Then back out into the streets they go,

back home to a world so different.

The lack of decent clothing, or a roof over their heads;

leaving their young minds incoherent.

We, as educators, expect each child

to be able to walk through those doors,

sit down, and be ready to learn.

Truth is,

sometimes, that's the last thing on their minds,

because yesterday's mistakes brought bruises unearned.

Maybe the child didn't get sleep that night,

they heard gunshots, or sirens, until early dawn

Maybe they spent that

night quivering in fear,

wondering if tomorrow they'd still have a home.

As much as we hate to accept it, the choices adults make

affect childrenmore than we could ever know.

The ill effects of life's despair

can sometimes stunt their growth.

Until a change starts to take place

within the older generation

so that we may set better examples

for our seeds.

The lack of good parenting

and a solid education

will forever leave our nation in need.

Tick Tock

Tick tock goes the sound of life's clock

as time passes by;

Soul mates dissipate as the purple rain falls

and doves cry.

My princess like persona leaves

Disney in awe of me.

Cruelty's poison causing me to sometimes fall into a deep sleep;

The sweet kiss of hope brushes against my lips

as I awaken into a new dawn,

a new moon, who's solar eclipse has

blocked out all of the pain.

When the sun begins to shine again

it brings forth a new light

that opens my inner eye to notice the outer

appearanceof the world

as it revolves around my center of gravity.

I stay rooted in my consciousness.

Sometimes my mind gets so occupied

with the signs and the uncertainties

of mankind that I have to press stop,

then rewind, damn, I should have DVR'd my thoughts

so that I could fast forward past

the foolishness that litters the streets of humanity,

but then I have to think that I would

only grow weak; whatever doesn't kill me

only makes me stronger

and to pass up life's challenges would stunt

my emotional and spiritual growth.

Tick tock goes the sound of life's clock

as time slows down I see myself standing still.

I have to pick it back up.

I have to pick up my time card and punch back into life

so that I can get paid for my work.

Slowly I start to move through the states of what

matters; a flowing existence, a solid foundation,

and I can see through my present

and into my future.

Tick, Tick, Tick...Tock....

My time is up....

I must make a decision

based on my religion

do I straddle the line,

or do I cut it with precision?

This is my vision,

to mold my dreams into their own reality show

so the world can see my potential

and what I have to offer....

The world is my ocean and I.....

I am ready to get my feet wet.

Emotionally Disconnected

Emotionally disconnected, life's pull-strings are hectic,

yet expected.

Various levels of uncertainties play across my mind.

Metaphorically inept to the mind's eye

which sees the untruths, but

never tells the "untold" for sake of

being let loose into a world of discontent.

Now if, no ifs, not ever, never let anyone,

man, or woman, get the better of you,

your heart, your soul, your mind.

I wasn't ever told how it would be,

but suddenly I see and for me it's not

easy, could not care less

about being set free.

So what, I don't really give a, what?!

I guess your ass is out of luck.

Easily can I remove the sun that shines

once in a while inside my heart.

Easily can I block the rain that brings

pain by shutting out all aspects of "it", that thing.

Corruptible to thy being,

so cruel a game it plays with the unexpected,

the emotionally neglected, I have this down right perfected.

Now what? Playing Shits and Ladders with

shaky climbers who can't even make it

to the damn top, get popped, get dropped,

it's all the same.

I hope you feel the pain I felt while

Walking in the rain, it's insane and you're totally to blame.

My quality of life leaves something, at times, to

be desired, but I am wired.

Wired to be strong, to stay strong, to live strong

in the midst of the overwhelming and the weak.

I'm quick to speak my mind at times

when I am feeling the need to be heard.

My words are like gold they are valuable and undeterred.

Maybe only to me, but that's how it should

be. You can't rely on others to make you happy.

All people let you down at some point in your life,

but you pick up the broken parts and mend

them with the love in your heart and save

your heart for you and only you.

Nobody else will value your gift better than

you are able to.

I speak the truth. The shakers and fakers

of loves wanna-be makers

take away from the reality of life's gall, which is all,

in a sense, who and what you call yourself.

At the end of the day it's all about

taking care of number one.

It's all about you when the day is done.

People will come into your life and pretend;

Pretend to be your friend, saying they will be

there until the end, but if that's the case "the end"

can be seen over and over again, what then?

I may have finally figured out what it's all about.

    This life dream, this love thing;

        Between these two things,

    Three strikes, forget it, I'm out.

A Revolution

The funny thing is, is that life is like a mirror.

Your circumstances allow you to get a glimpse,

a reflection of who you are.

The choices that you've made etching a

stamp of remembrance;

The present that you now live in,

your past creating a hindrance.

As your doppelganger stares back and raises

a finger to point and laugh;

Your future looking bleak as you continue

to look back.

Each tomorrow has come and gone, blending

quietly with the past;

How do you move forward, when every day,

the same person looks at you from the glass?

A change is in order, it's time to rise and begin anew.

It's time to shatter that same old reflection,

that old reflection wasn't really you.

Pick up the broken pieces and rearrange your face.

Throw out all of the garbage and let revision take its place.

Air out your dirty laundry so that

all your linen is clean.

Refold your magnitude of life strings so that

now your filth is unseen.

Forgive those who trampled over you and walked on by

without a care.

Forgive those who heard your cries and ignored you because

they didn't see you standing there.

The new you has risen and you should move forward

with your head held high.

You're not the person that you used to be

because now your spirit shines so bright.

For every painful past,

For every unanswered solution,

don't stand and do nothing,

for tomorrow could be your revolution.

A Beautiful Scar

A light has fallen upon the dark earth of my soul.

Opening the wound on an unpleasant sore;

The smell of infection invades the nostrils of my psyche;

the oozing and the pain causing tears to flow endlessly.

I never wanted to revisit such torture, such pain,

such embarrassment, but I was told I needed to heal.

The only way for me to be cleansed and to rid myself

of the corruption that made a home in my heart was to....

Open Pandora's box.........

Sometimes I want to close it back and forget it's there,

but all of the progress that I have made would be null and void.

No, I will continue to dig deeper until the entire wound

has been cleansed and medicated with new life.

I will live on, with a beautiful scar that will

remind me of how perfectly imperfect I am now.

INTIMACY

Explicit Content

My thoughts cannot be written.

Parental discretion would surely be warranted.

Every time I see you my mind turns to thoughts

too provocative to write down, let me count the

ways. Would it be bad to let me taste you;

to strip you naked so that I could take in your beauty?

What if I wanted to tie you down and

make you beg me to please you?

How about if I wanted to taste every part of you?

Let me show

you just how bad I can be.

What if I wanted to cover you in oil and rub my skin

against yours?

My thoughts cannot be written.

Parental discretion is certainly advised.

Every time I glance in your direction

my thoughts turn dirty and I can't help,

but to think

of the things that I could do to you.

Let me count the ways.

Toxic

The way that you hold me close

touching my body oh so right.

The love that you give me

makes me melt into a puddle of ecstasy.

You're all I need, day, or night

when things seem to go wrong,

you make everything all right.

You're all I want.

I can't seem to get enough.

There were times I tried

to walk away, but I still longed for

your touch.

The thought of losing you makes

me sick;

Because your love is so toxic.

Oceans

His waves gently swept along

her sandy beach.

His tide pulled shells that had been shattered by

trespassers

into his riptide; and he slowly

dipped them and twirled them.

He allowed his current to mold them into something

stunning.

The only thing that could rival it's

beauty is a pearl from the center of an oyster.

The cool ripple of his water cleansing her

shores and soothing her suntanned grains.

She wouldn't be who she is without him.

Together they create a lavish oasis of relaxation and

serenity.

The way they complement each other

and he touches her is remarkable;

a feeling that only the two of them

would ever understand.

At night, the moon sits above him,

crowning him like the king that he is.

She sits and watches as he stretches far and wide,

engulfing every inch of her.

She loves him, and he loves her;

and they unite in the salty air.

Only Time Will Tell

Only time will tell

where this relationship will go,

but I am willing to lie in your arms

and let you hold me close.

Without you, babe,

I have nothing, if you're

not here with me.

Your fingers gently stroking my skin and

your lips gliding over mine.

The love that emanates through you

from your heart to mine.

This whole life won't mean a thing

if I can't have you,

but if time pulled us apart,

you'd still have my heart.

Intimate Moment

We lie together and listen to each other breathe.

He strokes my face gently as I allow my fingers to

caress his biceps.

The look in his eyes causes a tear to slowly cascade down

my cheek.

I can see his heart.

I can see how much he loves and cares for me;

I can only hope that he can see the same.

I can only pray that he can glance into my windows

and understand how deeply he is rooted into my soul.

I place my hand over his heart

and I take his hand and place it over mine.

Our hearts were beating as one.

To be this close to him and to smell his scent always

seems to leave me intoxicated.

I slowly touch my lips to his and for the first time,

in our most intimate moment,

I was truly awake.

HIS

Unemotional Woman

Unemotional woman, what will it take to get through to you?

How can I make you understand that no other woman makes me feel the way that you do.

Unemotional woman, I've opened my heart and bared my soul to you.

I've told you my deepest fears and let my love for you bleed all over the floor and you give me nothing.

Unemotional woman I try every day to get to the root of your mind;

to express my everlasting desire to share my world with you until the end of time.

Unemotional woman you hurt my pride every time you shut me out.

I don't think you have a clue as to what a relationship is about.

I've tried many times to walk away.

I've tried many times to say I'm through, but there is

just something about who you are,

that makes me want to love only you.

Loves A Man

The smoothness of his skin,

despite the worries of his career.

The ripples across his abdomen

showing how much he cares about his health.

The muscles bulging from his biceps

proving the strength that he carries.

The broadness of his shoulders showing the world

he can withstand a heavy load.

The power in his hands,

allowing others to see he has a

grasp on life.

The sturdiness of his thighs and calves,

so that he can stand in the face of adversity.

His firmly planted feet, proof

that he is not easily shaken.

The sharp glare in his eyes,

that shows he demands to be seen.

The sharpness of his hearing,

so that he can be prepared for anything.

The quickness of his mind

as he prepares to speak on his beliefs.

The deep penetrating sound of his voice,

demanding respect from all who will listen.

These are only a few reasons,

that a woman loves a man.

I Want a Woman

I want a woman to match my intellect;

to understand that after a hard day's work

I need her to be my peace.

I want a woman who isn't afraid

to please her man mentally,

spiritually, emotionally, and sexually.

I want a woman to bare my seed

and to help turn my house into a home.

I want a woman who isn't afraid to strip

herself of the falsities of the world

and let her natural beauty shine forth.

I want a woman who is loving,

yet firm, and speaks her mind.

I want a woman who has a sense of humor;

a woman who will be my rock when I am weak.

I may not need a woman,

but I know exactly what I want.

I am willing to wait,

because I am a man and I deserve the best.

My Man

The strength of his arms and

the smell of his cologne.

Everything about him drives my senses wild.

There is nothing, nobody, at all like him.

His mental capacity is unlimited

and his work ethic is admirable.

His spirit shines forth and causes me

to be a better woman for myself and for him.

His desire to work hard and

to play even harder makes me want

to be near him all of the time.

The timber in his voice,

how his words melt off of his tongue

and drip into my ears

makes my body go into over drive

leaving me breathless.

This gorgeous specimen, this god-like being,

he is...........

my man.

Many Times

Many times he is expected to treat her

like a homie, lover, friend;

but what he sometimes needs is just a lover.

Sometimes, just a friend,

and every once in a while,

a homie,

but that is what his boys are for, right?

Many times he is expected

to be a protector, a provider, a "girlfriend";

but he feels that it's his job

to provide protection.

But why can't the two of you provide for each other?

Why does he have to be your "girl"?

Isn't that what your friends are for?

Women expect too much from men and sometimes

the list is just too long.

Why expect more from a man

than you are willing to offer?

HERS

I Am That Type of Woman

Yes, I am that type of woman
and I don't take no mess.
I can get it with the worst
and I can rock it with the best.
I have a swag that matches my style
and when I walk into a dark room,
it lights up when I smile.

Some may read this and think
that I am conceited, but I
really don't care because
I am confident in who I am
and what I am about.
If you were a woman like me,
you couldn't help but to stand and shout.

You have to love every inch of yourself;
you have to like you for who you are,
flaws and all,
and walk around with your head
held high, shoulders back, standing tall.

Yes, I am that type of woman,
I work, cook, and clean.
I can turn you on with more than just my intellect.
Don't mistake my kindness for weakness;
I have a big heart, but it can easily turn cold.
Yes, I am that type of woman, the one
that breaks the mold.

I know that my stubbornness is an issue,
my pride sometimes can cause me to fall.
I don't have a problem admitting
my faults, or when I'm wrong at all.

I know that I am not perfect and
yes I make mistakes, more than a few;
but yes, I am that type of woman.

You may not like it, but it is what it is.
You may not even see what I see and
You may not even feel how I feel,
but it doesn't matter, because I am
that type of woman, and that type of woman
is real.

A Choice

It happened so fast, so quickly

my mind could not comprehend.

I couldn't understand the painful grip of a man.

A man who said he loved me, he

let the words roll from his mouth.

His kind of love, filled my mind with doubt.

How often could he say

those three little words, those three

little words that mean so much;

but at the same time have hate come forth from his touch.

You see, I just don't get it,

I don't understand.

Once again, it is hard for me to comprehend.

He gave me material things, for those I had no need.

My needs were so much bigger, larger than his greens.

All I wanted was an ear, an ear to hear my voice,

but he chose to ignore me, and for that I made a choice.

I made my choice to leave that night,

to turn and walk away.

If I had to do it again,

I would make that same exact choice today.

Can You See Me?

Can you see me?

Can you see the pain inside of me?

At times I cry because it hurts so bad,

sometimes I laugh at myself for feeling so

damn sad.

The reason that I am angered,

the reason that I hurt;

Is because you don't see me

and walk all over me like dirt.

Why can't you see me?

I am standing right here. I am

standing here and you never stop and look.

You walk right on by me

as if our love was just a fluke.

Now I am standing alone, ignored by my one true love;

The one I thought was sent to me from

heaven up above.

Can you see me?

Hell no you can't see me!!

You never saw me, and you will never know the real me!!

So for that, I hate you!!

I never should have loved you!

You'll never find another woman

to do the things that I did for you.

I know that you don't care

it has always been my fault completely.

What matters now, even if you can't, I still see me!

Visions

Visions of a soul once battered,

stories untold of a spirit shattered.

I awake every day to face the

world which once, I confess,

I was flattered.

Day after day I sit and think,

Try to remember the days that I

missed.

So caught up in trying to stay

out of the way, trying to dodge

from being hit.

Night after night, I lay and cry,

using my tear soaked pillow

to dry my eyes.

So caught up in wanting to survive,

wanting to just live my life.

Visions of a soul once battered,

stories untold of a spirit shattered.

I wake up every day to face the world,

some days, wondering

if it even matters.

Here I am in this moment and

many years have now passed

since that fateful night

in December. Yet, here I sit unable to forget.

I know that I will always remember

The power that controlled him,

a liquid freedom that only he knew.

He never understood the damage he had done to me

physically, emotionally, and mentally

with every day that went by.

I am now beginning to become freer.

Visions of a soul once battered,

stories untold of a spirit shattered.

I wake up every day to face the world.

My desire to be strong,

to live life to the fullest,

to survive;

now that, is what matters.

Untitled

Things are not always what they seem.
Traveling along life's journey
brings many speed bumps and pot holes,
but we must keep going.
Storms come and go and
may even slow us down, or come
to a complete stop, but
that does not mean
that we should give up.
At times, that just means that we
may need a break, maybe even a detour.
As long as we end up at our destination
does it really matter?
A couple of wrong turns here and there
are inevitable, but as long as you
get back on track that is what counts.

JAE ELLE'S THOUGHTS

A Prayer

God,

  Please help me to have a more positive attitude on life and love. Please let me be able to look pass the little things and to not be easily angered, or get too emotional. Help me to be more logical, understanding, patient, and thoughtful. Lord, help me to be a better friend, fiancé, daughter, co-worker, etc. Please allow me to love more and judge less. Help me to be more understanding. Help me, oh Lord.

Amen

A Shield

  My emotions are my weakness. It causes a breakdown in my mind. I hide my heart from the world in order to shield it from getting battered and bruised. I shield my body from being ripped apart and abused. I put up my guard so that I can shield myself from getting hurt. You may not like me for keeping you out, but you haven't walked in my shoes, so you don't know what I'm about. If you choose to stick around, and watch as the bricks go tumbling to my feet, you will find a diamond in the rough and love me for being me.

Ain't It Funny

  It is so funny how people feel the need to get into relationships and down the line they start telling the person what they can and can't do. It is different if it is truly something that the person needs to change to make them better. I understand that totally and completely, but the minor things...get a grip. If a person does something that truly is who they are and it isn't going to disrupt the relationship, by all means..let them have it. There is no reason for them to change who they are. I believe most people realize this and that isn't where the problem lies. The problem comes, when person **A** starts telling person **B** what they should, or shouldn't be doing, but they do the EXACT same thing (pet peeve of mine). What is even funnier, is that as soon as they are called out about it they; a) justify why it is OK for them and why they should be able to keep doing it, or **b)** decide at that point just how important it is to "just be who you are", "just be yourself". My words for that, G.T.F. outta here please. Let me tell you this, ALWAYS be who you are. If you are with someone like that, let him or her know the deal. If it keeps happening, leave, ignore them, or get over it. People are all about voicing their opinions and attempting to put you on blast when their feelings get hurt, or something gets said to them. However, when the shoe is on the other foot they don't have anything to say, or they want to cover it up with something else. My thing is this; 1. Don't say anything to me if you are guilty of the same thing, 2. Don't tell me I'm wrong and give reasons why, but when I do the same to you, you try to justify why it's OK, and 3. Don't tell me to fix me when you need to be fixed and keep doing the same dumb shit. Remember, when you are pointing a finger at someone else, you have 3 pointing back at yourself.

Change

Change is so hard and to make it is always easier said than done. Especially when you already think you have been making some only to find out that isn't the case. With the right mindset and determination, it can be done. I don't know how I am going to do it, but I know that I am in need of making some. In truth, I am scared to death. I am terrified of it actually. I am frightened to the point of tears. However, some things are a must. It is necessary. It is detrimental to the person that you can become. I just hope that I prevail in the end. A challenge awaits. Please pray for me.

Divorces, Marriages, and Babies

Okay, look. I am happy that you're happy about your new found loves and kids on the way really, I am, but I don't need to hear about it every time you open your mouth. There are other things that go on in life. If you are getting divorced, I am sorry that you are having to go through that, trust me, I've been there and I know it's hard. My thing is, I can give advice, I don't mind at all, but what gets me is that when I ask you a question about your situation, answer it. Remember, you came to me for advice, so anything I ask, or say is fair game. If all you want me to do is listen then you better say that before you open your mouth because I'm going to give it to you like it is. Trust and believe that. Now, you people with the new relationships, good for you. I am glad that you've found someone that finally loves you, but don't make your world entirely about him or her because you never really know if that relationship will last. For those of you getting divorced, if that's what you really feel is best, then do it and stop making excuses as to why you can't. I did that too. If that's what you want, do it, as long as it's for the right reasons. You people having babies, CONGRATS, I'm happy for you, but once again, I don't need to hear about it all the time. If I ask how YOU are, I don't want to know about baby stuff. Why? Because I didn't ask you about it, that's why. Answer the question that I asked you. If you didn't want to have a kid, you should have taken the steps to prevent it and that goes for men and women. Don't get an attitude with me when I ask you why you didn't use protection. Don't get bothered when you say you didn't want him, or her to be the father, or mother and I ask you why you slept with them in the first place. I'm going to let that sink in....

Emotions on Ice

I hate the fact that I have emotions sometimes because they seem to cause more problems than they are worth. Being cold hearted seems like the way to go at times. I realize that being able to let your emotions flow at the appropriate times are okay, but it is those times that are inappropriate that make them hard to deal with. Not caring looks more and more attractive, but then I see that it's just not possible. It is just in my nature to care and even though I try to come across as this hard person at times...I'm really not. It is all just a defense mechanism that I use to cope through the pain and the anguish. Shutting myself off and holding things in is just my way of protecting my heart and my feelings from further damage. Some people care, but most people don't. Everyone wants to be there for you when times are great, but when you are down; nobody is there. I understand that everyone has problems and the last thing that they need is to add more to their issues by having to deal with someone else's. But, if you can be there for them, why can't they be there for you? It sounds like pure selfishness to me. I admit that I can be as stubborn as an ox and that I can let my pride get the best of me, but there are times that I feel like I don't have a choice. I feel that if I let down my guard too much I will either be taken advantage of, or I will be crushed beyond repair. So, I sit here at a crossroads because I don't know what to do.

Expectations

I fall short of your expectations every time. You make it clear that I'm not what you are to me. I turn in another direction in hopes of someone looking my way that will see me, like I see them. Is there such a thing? Does it exist?

God's Hedge of Protection

There is light in a place where darkness prevails even when it seems as if there is no hope. Some people fail to realize that at times you have to be your own light. You have to be that beaker of light to guide yourself through your darkest hour and sometimes you may end up having to be that light for someone else. I know that this can be a hard pill to swallow, especially on those days when it seems as if your light will never shine again, but that is when you have to remember that in your darkest hour, that is when God has put you in a place where you need to totally and completely surrender yourself to Him. Just like the one set of footprints from the story, He is carrying you even though you are so blinded by the darkness that you can't see Him. He is still covering you with a hedge of protection. Even though it seems that you are alone, you aren't. When you finally figure out a way to be able to keep God's hedge up and in good condition, you will rest easy through those trying times. You will find, instead of tearing it down because you think that it is in your way, you will be able to welcome it with your faith. If you nurture it properly, it will always be there. In order to maintain that hedge of protection, you need to make sure that your roots are deeply planted (How deeply are you rooted in the Word of God?), you are watering it every day (Are you showering God with the praise He deserves?), and make sure you are letting enough sun in (Do you have a relationship with the Son?). When all of these components are in place, you will forever be protected by God's grace and the darkness won't be an issue.

How Can You Tell Someone Is Right For You?

If you are with someone and you are wondering if that person is meant for you, chances are, they aren't. The reason I say this, is because if you are with someone that you truly love and care about, you can feel it. There isn't any doubt in your mind. You enjoy being with that person and you love that person for who, and what, they are (flaws and all). Every person has the potential to be great, but you have to make sure that the both of you are prepared for it. If the timing is off, or even the situation, you may need to step back and examine what is really going on. If the timing is wrong, the relationship will not work. You can't go off of a wing and a prayer, or a possibility. You don't know what the future holds so why even stagnate your life for something that isn't guaranteed? What would it serve you to put your life on hold? That would, in effect, put you way out of balance with your partner, or your "possible" future partner. Relationships work among equals. You don't want to start pining over a possibility because it can go in either direction. It's good if it works out, but what if it doesn't. That is time that you are unable to get back. Time that could have been spent doing something productive with your life, and theirs. You should just go for what is real, what is concrete. Don't get sucked into a fantasy because your life is a reality.

Is It Worth It?

Let me talk about relationships. Naturally, there are many different kinds. You have the relationships with friends, parents, siblings, co-workers, associates, enemies, but the most sought after, a partner. Why? Humans, hell, animals in general, seek some sort of companionship. They want to feel that closeness with someone. There are many great things that happen as a result of relationships; Marriage, kids, financial stability (in some cases), and someone to encourage you. Those are only a few of the good things. Of course, there are downfalls as well. Then there is the bickering, the jealousy (in some cases), and just the flat out drama of two different people trying to co-exist. The question I would like to raise is this. Is it really worth it?

Life

Every now and then life hits us with the unexpected. It is during those times that we must dig our heels in deep and stand firm within our faith and become unmovable. It won't be easy by any means, but learning how to weather the storm and fight when we feel like giving up will only make us stronger in the end. It isn't the falling down that gets people, it's the staying down. We must learn how to pick ourselves back up each time that we fall and start again. Getting knocked backwards gives us that much more room to get a running start so that we may leap farther.

Married vs. Single

I have learned that marriage is all about sacrifice and commitment. It has to be mutual, though. In the beginning I was sad at the thought of my marriage ending but happy to finally have my life back. I know what it's like to be in an unhappy marriage. I know what it is like to live with a controlling spouse. I have learned that being married is about compromising and making decisions together. But what do you do if your spouse refuses to see that and refuses to let you make any decisions? That is something that I missed about being single, well, I guess I never really was until after I left. I encourage you, if you are single, to embrace it and enjoy it. If you are married I sincerely hope that you are happy. I am unsure as to whether or not I will ever get married again, but I do think single life doesn't look as bad as some people make it out to be. I never wanted to get married in the first place and I shocked myself when I did. Now that I am not anymore, I am pretty content. I don't totally regret my marriage only because I learned a lot about myself and about relationships. I thank God that I didn't have any kids at that point in time and I am not sure if I want any. Don't get me wrong. I love kids. I really do I mean, that's one of the reasons I am a teacher, but to have my own is different. So many people say that I will want kids when the right man comes along and I am sure that may be true, but right now I don't see it. People play to many games with other peoples' hearts and emotions. I don't have time for that. For those who are so set on finding someone, relax, it will happen when it happens. For those who are married, I hope that it's all that you hoped it would be. For those who are single, get out there and live it up and forget about all of the other mess.

Me

I need to make a way to becoming a better me. I have made so much progress. I have come a long way, but see, sometimes, I just don't know because I let my emotions run free. I struggle with how to rein them in and when to let them be. Maybe I should stay prayer focused and stay on one accord with God because I am unsure about what else to do to rid myself of these internal flaws. I need to find a way to cope, I need to dig deep and locate the root so that I may be able to easily cleanse myself and be a better woman completely. Nobody can help me in my journey, not you, just me.

My Black America (Written in 2009)

Even in the year 2009 with an African American president, racism is still very much alive and kicking. Although some may not see it every day, it is still there. Sometimes, for those who are not of color, it may even be easily overlooked, or flat out ignored, but believe me, it's there. As a young woman, I still remember my first racist encounter with a white, female sales associate when I was a teenager. I was in the mall shopping with family and I had wandered off alone. I started browsing a few of the department store racks and out of the corner of my eye I noticed her standing a couple of racks away, and she was pretending to straighten them. I had a feeling that she was watching me, but I figured that I was just being paranoid so I continued walking around and looking. After a few minutes, I began to realize that she was indeed following me around the store to make sure I wasn't going to steal anything. I remember getting angry and asking her what the h*** her problem was and assuring her that she was wasting her time following me around. She quickly tried to explain that she wasn't following me, but I just turned and walked away. After that experience, I became more aware of the fact that, despite how far we have come as a nation, racism has yet to be silenced. Although it is now a whisper, sometimes, that's the worst kind. Since then, I haven't had to worry too much about racism. The other night, I had a rude awakening. I was on my way home from eating an early dinner and I saw flashing lights in my rear view mirror. I knew I hadn't been speeding so I immediately became uncomfortable. When I pulled over, I rolled down my window and then reached for my license and registration. While I was getting my information together to present to the officer, he flashed his light into my car and asked me what I was doing. I told him that I was getting my information ready to give him. With an attitude he said to me, "I didn't ask you for it". I was taken aback at how rude his tone was. I simply said 'okay' and sat back. He then asked me to step out of the car. I asked him why and he told me to just do it. I refused and reminded him that he was supposed to ask for my information, run it, and then, if it was necessary, ask me to get out of the car. He told me to stop being smart and to get out of the car. I still refused to move. At that point he opened my door and reached for my seat belt, so I decided to go ahead and get out. I was standing next to my car and he reaches in and gets my information. I was standing in the cold night air mumbling about how I couldn't believe this was happening to me. The cop overheard me and asked me what I said. I told him and he said, "Believe it". Out of anger I just shook my head and snorted. He then came back over and said that I needed to have a seat. Assuming he meant for me to sit in my car, I was walking back over to my front seat to sit down. He had other plans. He told me to turn around and put my hands behind my back. Confused, I asked why, I hadn't done anything. Again he told me to turn around. Thinking about all of the horror stories that I had heard on the news, I complied. He then cuffed me and sat me in the back of his squad car. I sat there as he proceeded to run my information. When he was done, he took me out of the car, walked me to mine and took the cuffs off. I asked him what the problem was and all he said to me was, "You fit the description of someone we are looking for". Yeah, right. Welcome to my Black America.

Never Forget

Many times people become so consumed by their day-to-day activities that they fail to stop and "smell the flowers". Life is such a rat race that many are busy chasing the almighty dollar, or so focused on staying busy that they neglect those things, which are most important such as family, friends, and just enjoying what life has to offer. Try to take time out of each day to just sit and listen. Sit and pray, write, read, or whatever it is that you do to unwind. Then, just talk. Talk to God, or talk to those who are close to you. You never know when the last breath you take will indeed be your last.

Pray

Sometimes it seems as if we go through more bad things than good things in life. If this is the case, ask yourself, what am I praying for? If you are praying for strength, God will send trials that build you up. If you are praying for patience, He will throw in trials that will make you have to wait. If you want financial stability, He will see just how faithful you can be with paying your tithes and managing your money. Be careful what you pray for because you have to make sure that you are ready to "go through", to "get to".

Priorities vs. Preferences: And the Winner Is?

Priority: *b (1)*: superiority in rank, position, or privilege**Preference:** *b* : the power or opportunity of choosing

Many people have this idea of the perfect person that they want to be with. In a previous blog I spoke about how there is no such thing as a perfect person, but there is most definitely a perfect person FOR you. We all have our preferences about what we would like our mates to have and a sane person is even willing to sacrifice some of those preferences for love. At some point in time, however, people have to come to terms with the fact that just because a person looks good, that doesn't mean that they are good for you. A real man, or woman, will have goals set and their priorities in order. They will realize then, that they are going to need a person that will complement those goals and priorities (and vice versa). Preference or priority? Many people need to think about what they really find to be most important to them.

Focus On You

Sometimes you sit and think about why people do the things that they do, or say the things that they say. I have found myself in deep thought about this and realize that people are who they are and there is nothing anyone can do about it. With that said, you can't change other people. When you are in a relationship with someone (boyfriend/girlfriend, friendship, family, etc.) do not, and I repeat, DO NOT try to change them. I made the mistake of staying in a past relationship far too long hoping that I could change him. Even though I was trying to change him for the better, I wore myself down because of it. You can't change anyone that doesn't want to change for themselves.

We, as women, tend to be the nurturers and the peacemakers. Unfortunately, that doesn't always work. We have to learn how to let go and let things be what they are. If we get too wrapped up in trying to change someone else, we will lose ourselves in the process. So, instead of focusing on them, focus on you and the positive things that you can bring to the table.

The House that Love Built

To understand the way that love works, my best friend came up with an analogy. He equated it with a house and its foundation. I further helped him to elaborate on it and this is what we came up with. When someone builds their home from the ground up, they must start with a sturdy foundation if they want their house to survive the rain and the storms. In a relationship, communication, trust, sex (yes sex), sacrifice, compromise, etc., all of these characteristics help to build a solid foundation in a relationship. The house that sits on top of that foundation is Love. When all of these characteristics are set in place, and two individuals fall in love with each other, they start to build their love for each other on the foundation that they have created. If any of these things were to be damaged in the relationship, then the house becomes unsteady. Cracks start to form in the foundation and the house shifts. Now, the love (house) is still there, but underneath, where you can't see it from the outside (the foundation), it isn't stable. If all of these things start to crumble and fall apart, then the house will fall. Even though the foundation has crumbled and the house has fallen, the wood, shingles, glass, etc. (all the pieces that it took to build your love for each other) are still there, but they are now in another form. A form that is no longer attractive. At that point, the house is now in a state that you two are unable to live in. With that said, you have a few choices: 1. Repair those cracks before your house falls apart, 2. If your house has fallen, take the time, and the money to re-build your foundation and your home, or 3. If you both know that the foundation is in the process of crumbling and neither of you wants the house anyway, then both of you, or one of you, needs to find a new place to live.

What is Love?

What is love? How do you show love? How should love be received? These are questions that have been haunting humanity for as long as humans have existed. The answer? It depends on the individual. I know that isn't the answer that most people would like to hear, but it is the truth. What may define love for me may be different for someone else. The way that I would like love to be presented to me, someone else may want it presented to them in a totally different light. So the questions that need to be asked are...What is love to me? How do I show love? How do I want to receive love?

What You Put Out, Is What You Get In

Many times people try to act so upset and confused when they get approached in certain ways. Yes, I do believe that there are just flat out idiots out there who don't get the picture, but there are those that cause things to happen to themselves. Don't point fingers, because men AND women both do it. If you are dressing provocatively all of the time, yes, things are going to get said and God forbid, something could even happen to you, but it goes farther than just dress. It also goes with the way that you talk to people and the things that you say. If you are constantly talking about sex with people and putting it all out in public, let's face it, don't be surprised if you get dubbed a "garden tool". Hey, if it quacks like a duck and looks like a duck, well, do I need to finish it?

Another issue that falls under this category is how people think that it's OK for them to do, and say, whatever they want when they want and don't expect anything to happen, or get said back to them. NEGATIVE. If you are going to put out some BS, expect to get it back, especially from me. I can't stand it when someone thinks they just know it all, when in reality, they are just a bunch of hot air. Please, spare us all and keep your mouth closed. We don't want to hear it. Next, if you make sideways comments, act sneaky, withhold information just because you get mad, tell half of the story, etc., guess what you are? You are my home girl's favorite word, SUSPECT!! Yeah, I said it. Especially when everyone and their mama know what your M.O. is. We aren't stupid. Men are great at this one, and yeah, there are a few pro females out there, too. Trust me boo, you aren't fooling anyone. If you are concerned about what people think of you, if it really is that big of a deal, then you should try to be on your P's and Q's at all times. If you're not, then continue to do you and don't question what people do, or say to you. I'm just saying.

Afterward

Now that you have come to the end of Volume 1, I would like to thank you for taking the time to delve into my heart, mind, and soul. I pray that you really enjoyed my book and I also hope that you were able to connect with many of my thoughts and poems. For a peak at my upcoming works please visit the following:

My website: www.atmspeaks.com

Facebook: And The Mind Speaks

Twitter: @atmspeaks

Tumblr: atmspeaks

Instagram: ricksnation

E-Mail: atmspeaks@gmail.com

www.ingramcontent.com/pod-product-compliance
Lightning Source LLC
Chambersburg PA
CBHW061334040426
42444CB00011B/2918